Contents

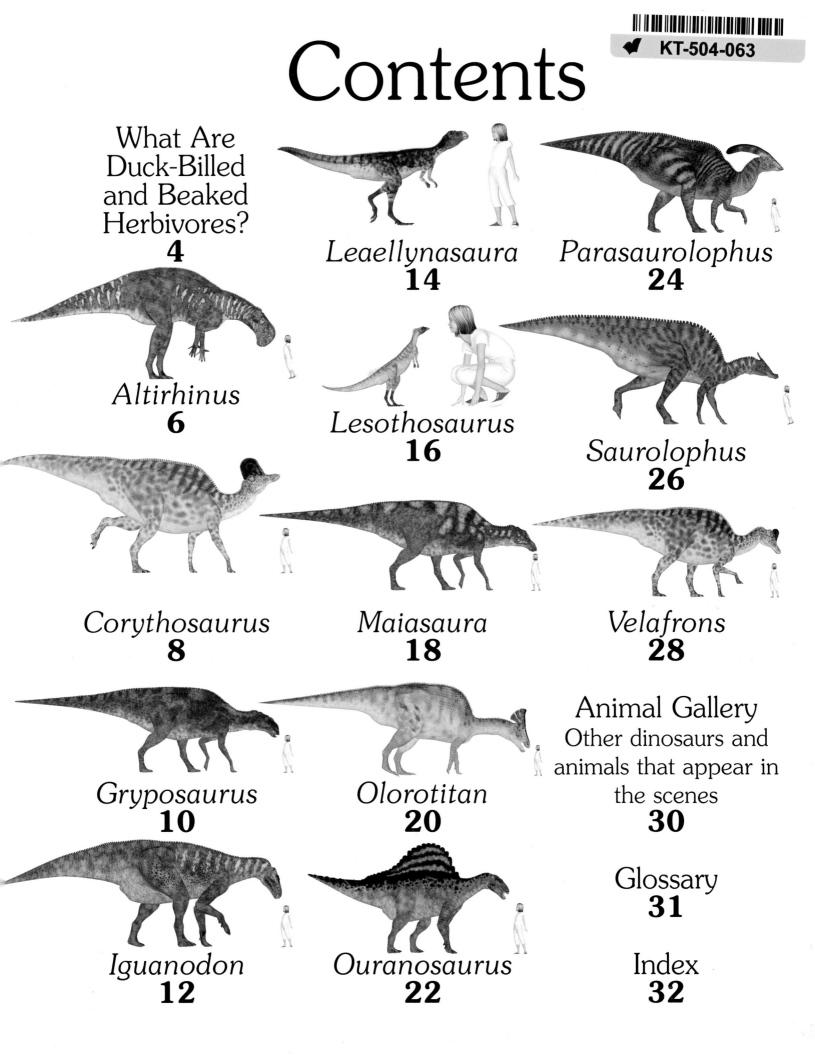

*The dinosaurs here are of three different types. Parasaurolophus is a **hadrosaurid**, Iguanodon is an **iguanodont**, and Lesothosaurus is an **ornithopod**.*

SELF DEFENCE
With the exception of the iguanodonts' thumb spikes (*see pp. 12–13*), these dinosaurs had no defence against **predators**, relying on herding to provide safety in numbers. The smaller ornithopods used speed to escape their attackers.

What Are Duck-Billed and Beaked **Herbivores**?

Duck-billed dinosaurs belonged to the family hadrosauridae, whose members were plant eaters with duck bill-shaped beaks. They were related to iguanodontian dinosaurs and had similar body layouts. Along with iguanodonts and hadrosaurids, smaller beaked dinosaurs are included to make up the group known as ornithopods.

*Dinosaurs lived throughout the Mesozoic Era, which is divided into three periods, shown here. It is sometimes called the Age of the Reptiles. Dinosaurs first appeared in the Upper Triassic period and died out during a **mass extinction event** 65 million years ago.*

DINO URS!

PARASAUROLOPHUS
AND OTHER DUCK-BILLED AND
BEAKED HERBIVORES

by
David West

W

FRANKLIN WATTS
LONDON•SYDNEY

This edition 2015
First published in the UK in 2013 by Franklin Watts

Franklin Watts
338 Euston Road
London NW1 3BH

Franklin Watts Australia
Level 17/207 Kent Street
Sydney, NSW 2000

Dewey classification: 567.9'14

A CIP catalogue record for this book is available from the British Library.

ISBN: 978 1 4451 4038 4

Franklin Watts is a division of Hachette Children's Books, an Hachette UK company.
www.hachette.co.uk

DINOSAURS! PARASAUROLOPHUS and other DUCK-BILLED and BEAKED HERBIVORES
was produced for Franklin Watts by
David West Children's Books, 6 Princeton Court, 55 Felsham Road, London SW15 1AZ

Designed and illustrated by David West

Printed in China

CRESTS

Hadrosaurids are divided into two sub-families. The lambeosaurines had hollow head crests and were generally less bulky. The hadrosaurines, like *Maiasaura* (see pp. 18–19), had no crests and were usually larger.

Parasaurolophus

BILLS AND BEAKS

Hadrosaurids had beaks that looked like a duck's bill, which is why they are called duck-billed dinosaurs. Iguanodonts and the smaller ornithopods had narrow skulls with a toothless beak that was covered in a horn-like material called keratin. At the back of the jaws were **batteries** of teeth for mashing up the tough plants they fed on.

Iguanodon

Lesothosaurus

FOUR OR TWO-LEGGED

The bulky hadrosaurids and iguanodonts could walk on two or four legs. The smaller ornithopods were two-legged and very quick in order to escape predators.

SIZE

Both duck-bills and iguanodonts grew to enormous sizes. *Iguanodon* reached 8.8 metres (29 feet) and *Parasaurolophus* could grow to 9.4 metres (31 feet). *Lesothosaurus* was only 1 metre (3.3 feet).

227	205	180	159	144		98		65 Millions of years ago (mya)
Upper	Lower	Middle	Upper		Lower		Upper	
TRIASSIC		JURASSIC			CRETACEOUS			

Altirhinus

Altirhinus means 'high nose'. It was closely related to
Iguanodon (see pp. 12–13). *Altirhinus* differed from
Iguanodon only in that it had more teeth, a flatter,
wider bill and a very curved nose.

The arched nose of *Altirhinus* may have been able to expand for
courtship display, as in modern-day **elephant seals**. *Altirhinus* was
two-legged when walking or running, but probably became four-legged
when feeding from the ground. The three middle fingers of its hand

A group of Altirhinuses *feed on the few plants at the edge of a desert in this scene from Lower Cretaceous Asia. A herd of Altirhinus can be seen in the background,* **migrating** *to greener feeding grounds.*

were wide and ended in hoof-like bones, suggesting that they were used for walking. The outside fingers were different. The first finger was a sharp spike, as on *Iguanodon*. Besides defence, the thumb spike might also have been used for breaking the shells of seeds or fruit. The fifth finger may have been useful for grasping food. *Altirhinus* could crop with its beak while chewing with its teeth.

Altirhinus was about 8.5 metres (28 feet) long and weighed around 3.6 metric tons (4 tons).

Corythosaurus

Corythosaurus was a type of duck-billed or hadrosaurid dinosaur called a lambeosaurine. Its name means 'helmet lizard', referring to the large semi-circular crest growing up from its head. It was closely related to *Lambeosaurus* and *Olorotitan* (see pp. 20–21), although their crests were very different.

Like other duck-billed dinosaurs, it had a toothless beak, which it used to pluck plant leaves and stems. The back of the jaws contained

8

A group of Corythosauruses *make their way to a water hole in this scene from Upper Cretaceous North America. A male calls out a signal using his crest to **amplify** the sound. Males might have had coloured crests for courtship display.*

hundreds of small teeth. These were used to crush and grind plants. When a tooth wore down, it was replaced by a newly grown tooth. As with other lambeosaurines, *Corythosaurus*'s crest contained air passages that were connected to its nose and lungs. They made sounds like a loud wind instrument that might have been used at times of danger.

Corythosaurus grew up to 10.7 metres (35 feet) long and weighed around 3.6 metric tons (4 tons).

Gryposaurus

Gryposaurus, meaning 'hooked-nose lizard' because of the shape of its nose, was one of the most widely spread and longest-lived hadrosaurids. These dinosaurs lived across the entire North American continent for five million years.

This dinosaur gets its name from the distinctive bony bump on its nose. The roughened texture of the bump suggests that it may have been used to butt other males during mating competitions.

A herd of Gryposauruses *crosses a narrow river to better feeding grounds, while a pair of* Chirostenotes *look on in this scene from Upper Cretaceous North America. A male* Gryposaurus *in the foreground shows off his coloured nose in a courtship* **ritual**.

A cast taken from fossilised remains shows that the skin on its neck, sides and belly was covered with scales less than 0.6 centimetre (0.25 inch) in size. *Gryposaurus* had a huge array of 300 teeth, which were replaced when they wore out. Scientists think it was able to eat any type of plants, using its beak to rip away tough stems while its teeth mashed food into a pulp.

Gryposaurus was about 10 metres (33 feet) long and weighed up to 2.7 metric tons (3 tons).

11

Iguanodon

Iguanodon means 'iguana tooth', because its teeth looked like those of an iguana. It was one of the earliest dinosaur **fossils** to be discovered, even before the name 'dinosaur' was used. An early mistake in reconstruction placed its thumb spike on its nose!

Iguanodon's body structure was quite similar to that of its later relatives, the hadrosaurids. It could shift from walking on two legs to walking on four. Its arms were long and strong, with hands that had three central

12

Its thumb spikes useless against the fast-moving predators, a sickly Iguanodon *struggles to stay on its feet as a pack of* Deinonychuses *snap and slash at it in this scene from Lower Cretaceous North America.*

fingers ending in hooves that could bear weight. The thumbs were conical spikes that stuck out and were possibly used as defensive weapons. The little finger was long and could have been used to hold plants while feeding. The front end of the snout was like a beak that was used to crop plants. The many broad teeth in the back of the jaw mashed up the plants.

Iguanodon grew up to 8.8 metres (29 feet) long and weighed around 3.2 metric tons (3.5 tons).

Leaellynasaura

Leaellynasaura was named after the daughter of the **paleontologist** who discovered it. Its fossils were found in south-eastern Australia, but when *Leaellynasaura* was alive, the continent was much farther south, inside the Antarctic Circle.

Leaellynasaura was a small ornithopod dinosaur that weighed slightly more than a child. It lived in Antarctica where, for part of the year, there was no sunlight. The climate was warmer 110 million years ago,

14

A pair of Leaellynasauras *run back to their burrows across sandy dunes near the coast of a Lower Cretaceous South Polar continent. The sun barely rises above the horizon as the long dark days of winter approach.*

but was still relatively cold, especially during the dark days of winter. The eyes of *Leaellynasaura* were huge, and the part of the brain controlling sight was large. This suggests it was well **adapted** to living in a dark environment. Scientists think it may have been warm-blooded, since there are no modern, cold-blooded reptiles living in arctic environments.

Leaellynasaura grew to about 2.1 metres (7 feet) long and weighed up to 16.3 kilogrammes (36 pounds).

15

Lesothosaurus

Lesothosaurus, meaning 'Lesotho lizard', was named after the country its fossils were found in. It had short arms, a long tail and long legs that made it a fast runner. Like other ornithopods, it needed to be speedy to escape predators such as *Syntarsus*.

Lesothosaurus had a small beak with which to crop tough plants. Behind the beak, it had flat, triangular-shaped teeth that interlocked. These were good for chewing up the plants it fed on.

A group of Lesothosauruses *scatter across a sandy beach to escape a speedy* **carnivorous** Syntarsus *in this coastal scene from Upper Triassic Africa. Parts of* Lesothosaurus's *skeleton were hollow, indicating that it was a light and fast dinosaur.*

The skeleton of *Lesothosaurus* was light. Its leg and arm bones were hollow, and there were hollow spaces in the skull. The front limbs were small, and the hands each had four big fingers and a smaller fifth finger, which were probably used for grasping plants while it ate. While browsing on plants, *Lesothosaurus* might occasionally stand upright and scan the landscape for prowling predators.

Lesothosaurus grew to 1 metre (3.3 feet) long and weighed about 6 kilogrammes (13 pounds).

Maiasaura

Maiasaura, meaning 'caring mother lizard', was a large hadrosaurine with a flat, wide beak. It was named after nests were discovered with remains of eggshells and babies too large to be **hatchlings**. This suggested that these giant dinosaurs raised their young.

Herds of *Maiasauras* built nesting **colonies** that were packed closely together, like those of seabirds today. The nests were made of soil, with gaps between them of around 7 metres (23 feet), less than the

18

In this scene from Upper Cretaceous North America, a nesting colony of Maiasauras includes hatchlings scampering about while others are being fed in their nest by their parents. An approaching sandstorm threatens to bury the colony.

length of the adult dinosaur. The eggs were laid in a circular pattern, up to 40 at a time. Fossils of baby *Maiasauras* show that they were unable to walk when they first hatched. Fossils also show that their teeth were partly worn, because the adults fed them in the nest. They had large eyes and a short snout, giving them a cute appearance – a common feature among animals that rely on their parents.

Maiasaura grew up to 9.1 metres (30 feet) long and weighed up to 3.6 metric tons (4 tons).

Olorotitan

Olorotitan, meaning 'gigantic swan', was named for its long, swan-like neck. It is the most complete hadrosaur fossil ever to be found outside North America. It had an unusual crest in the shape of a fan growing out of the back of its head.

Like *Corythosaurus* (see pp. 8–9), *Olorotitan* used its crest both as a sound instrument and as a device to attract females during courtship. Like other lambeosaurines, it had a beak to pluck plants and a battery

A group of Olorotitans *have moved down to a pool fed by a waterfall in this scene from Upper Cretaceous Asia. Places such as these, with the* **potential** *for sudden flooding, were ideal for the fossilisation of dead animals as they quickly became buried in silt.*

of teeth at the back of its jaw to crush the food before swallowing. *Olorotitan* was closely related to the North American lambeosaurines *Corythosaurus* and *Hypacrosaurus*. Scientists think that these lambeosaurines originally came from the area we know as Asia and migrated to North America before the large land mass split into several continents.

Olorotitan grew to 11.9 metres (39 feet) and weighed about 2 metric tons (2.2 tons).

21

Ouranosaurus

Ouranosaurus means 'brave lizard'. It was very strange looking, with tall spines growing from its back. Scientists think these may have supported a hump like a camel's or a sail-like structure. The sail would have helped regulate its body temperature in a warm climate.

Paleontologists think that *Ouranosaurus* lived in a harsh, almost desert-like environment and was closely related to *Iguanodon* (see pp. 12–13). They had many similar features, such as a thumb spike, which

22

Three Ouranosauruses, *who have become separated from their herd, make their way across a rocky desert in search of green feeding grounds in this scene from Lower Cretaceous Africa. One* Ouranosaurus *stops to call out to its lost herd.*

was smaller on *Ouranosaurus*. Its wrist was large, and the bones were fused together, which made it stronger when walking. The second and third fingers were broad and hoof-like, and the last outside finger was long and probably used for holding leaves and twigs. It had an unusual head, and its snout, which was much longer than *Iguanodon*'s, ended in a beak.

Ouranosaurus was about 7 metres (23 feet) long and weighed around 2.4 metric tons (2.7 tons).

23

Parasaurolophus

Parasaurolophus means 'like *Saurolophus*' (see pp. 26–27). It was a lambeosaurine, and its most noticeable feature was its long head crest. There are three species, all with different-sized crests. *Parasaurolophus walkeri*, shown here, had the longest crest.

There were many theories about the crest's function. One was that it was used as a snorkel to help with underwater breathing. This has now been rejected, since there is no hole at the end of the crest. It is

24

In a scene from Upper Cretaceous North America, a herd of Parasaurolophuses *moves on from a water hole. The male* Parasaurolophuses *are reddening and using their head crests to sing in a courtship contest.*

believed that the head crest may have had several uses. It was used as a visual display for identifying species and sex. Hollow tubes inside suggest that it was also used to amplify sound. These duck-bills also had good hearing, and experiments have shown that adults were sensitive to the high frequencies a **juvenile** might produce. It has also been suggested that the crest may have been used to keep the brain cool.

Parasaurolophus was about 9.4 metres (31 feet) long and weighed up to 5.4 metric tons (6 tons).

25

Saurolophus

Saurolophus, or 'crested lizard', was a large hadrosaurine dinosaur. It is one of the few dinosaurs found on more than one continent. It is recognised by a spike-like crest that sticks up and back from its head. Like all hadrosaurs, it could walk on four or two legs.

As with *Parasaurolophus* (see pp. 24–25), the head crest might have had several functions. Fossils were found in the Horseshoe Canyon Formation, close to the **encroaching** Western Interior Seaway, the

As rolling waves crash against a headland, a group of Saurolophuses make their way along the rocky shore of the Western Interior Seaway of Upper Cretaceous North America. In the background, Pteranodons glide above the waves in search of fish.

shallow sea that covered the mid-section of North America through much of the Cretaceous period. *Saurolophus* lived with hadrosaurids *Edmontosaurus* and hollow-crested *Hypacrosaurus*, **hypsilophodont** *Parksosaurus*, **ankylosaurid** *Euoplocephalus*, **nodosaurid** *Edmontonia*, horned dinosaur *Pachyrhinosaurus*, **pachycephalosaurid** *Stegoceras*, and the ostrich-mimic *Ornithomimus*.

Saurolophus grew up to 11.9 metres (39 feet) long and weighed around 1.9 metric tons (2.1 tons).

Velafrons

Velafrons, meaning 'sailed forehead', is a newly named dinosaur whose fossil remains were recently discovered in Mexico. It was a large plant eater belonging to the lambeosaurine family of duck-bills.

Velafrons lived in a humid estuary near the southernmost tip of Laramidia, a part of western America at the edge of the Western Interior Seaway. It was an area where salt water from the ocean mixed with freshwater from rivers. Many of the fossilised dinosaur bones

In this scene from Upper Cretaceous western America, a pair of Velafronses *are caught by a large wave as a giant storm brews up out at sea. Whole herds of dinosaurs could be wiped out by these* **catastrophic** *storms.*

discovered with *Velafrons* are covered with fossilised snails and marine clams, suggesting that *Velafrons* lived near the shore. The region was sometimes hit by huge, violent storms that affected miles of coastline and killed off entire herds of dinosaurs. Scientists think that *Velafrons*'s crest would have been used as a musical instrument for attracting females.

Velafrons grew up to 10.9 metres (35.7 feet) long and weighed up to 1.6 metric tons (1.8 tons).

Animal Gallery

Other dinosaurs and animals that appear in
the scenes.

Pteranodon (pp. 26–27)
'toothless flyer'
pterosaur (flying reptile)
Upper Cretaceous
United States

Deinonychus (p. 13)
'terrible claw'
carnivorous
dromaeosaurid
(vicious **raptor**)
Lower Cretaceous
United States

Chirostenotes
(pp. 10–11)
'narrow-handed'
oviraptorosaur
(beaked, feathered raptor)
Upper Cretaceous
Canada

Syntarsus (pp. 16–17)
'fused ankle'
theropod (two-legged
carnivorous dinosaur)
Upper Triassic
South Africa, United States,
Zimbabwe

Glossary

adapted Changed to cope with a different condition or situation.

amplify To make a sound louder.

ankylosaurid A member of the ankylosauridae family of armoured dinosaurs that includes *Ankylosaurus*.

batteries Rows or a grouping in lines.

carnivorous Meat eating.

catastrophic Violent and destructive.

colonies Groups of animals of the same species that live closely with each other.

courtship Mate-selection rituals.

dromaeosaurid A member of a group of carnivorous dinosaurs known as raptors, with slashing claws on their feet.

elephant seals Elephant seals take their name from the large inflating nose of the adult males, which looks like a short elephant's trunk.

encroaching Moving over boundaries, as when deserts encroach on grassland.

fossils The remains of living things that have turned to rock.

hadrosaurid A member of the family of duck-billed dinosaurs called *hadrosauridae*.

hatchling The newborn animal that emerges from a hard-shelled egg.

herbivore A plant eater.

hypsilophodont A member of a family of fast, herbivorous, small, two-legged ornithopod dinosaurs.

iguanodont A member of the plant-eating dinosaurs that include *Iguanodon*.

juvenile A young dinosaur.

mass extinction event A large-scale disappearance of animal and plant species over a relatively short period of time.

migrating Moving from one place to another, either for a short seasonal period, or for ever.

nodosaurid A member of a family of ankylosaurian dinosaurs.

ornithopod A member of the ornithopoda family of bird-hipped dinosaurs that became one of the most successful groups of plant-eating dinosaurs in the Cretaceous world.

pachycephalosaurid A member of a family of bone-headed dinosaurs that includes *Pachycephalosaurus*.

paleontologist A scientist who studies the forms of life that existed in earlier geological periods by looking at fossils.

potential To have the possibility.

predators Animals that hunt and kill other animals for food.

pterosaur A member of the flying reptiles that lived during the age of the dinosaurs.

raptors Members of the family dromaeosauridae, such as *Deinonychus*.

rituals A series of special acts or ways of doing something.

theropod A member of a two-legged dinosaur family that includes most of the giant carnivorous dinosaurs.

Index